salmonpoetry

Diverse Voices from Ireland and the World

dismantle

poems by
anne tannam

salmonpoetry

Published in 2024 by
Salmon Poetry
Cliffs of Moher, County Clare, Ireland
Website: www.salmonpoetry.com
Email: info@salmonpoetry.com

Copyright © Anne Tannam, 2024

ISBN 978-1-915022-58-5

All rights reserved. No part of this publication may be reproduced or transmitted in any form or by any means, electronic or mechanical, including photography, recording, or any information storage or retrieval system, without permission in writing from the publisher. The book is sold subject to the condition that it shall not, by way of trade or otherwise, be lent, resold or otherwise circulated without the publisher's prior consent in any form of binding or cover other than that in which it is published and without a similar condition, including this condition, being imposed on the subsequent purchaser.

Cover & Title Page Image: Darragh Murphy (aj_axis)
Cover Design & Typesetting: Siobhán Hutson
Author Photo: Neil Murphy

Printed in Ireland by Sprint Print

Salmon Poetry gratefully acknowledges the support of
The Arts Council / An Chomhairle Ealaíon

for Claire, Aislinn, Sian and Darragh

Contents

existence	9
child **as**	13
dismantle	14
origin story	15
one of these days	16
notional	17
conjure	18
before the fall	19
little girl	20
when you leave	21
out in the world	22
meanwhile	23
night vision	24
my beloved	25
hanging by a thread	29
man **as**	30
tell me again	31
those boys you used to teach	32
diviner	33
interview	34
prodigal	35
mother **as**	39
wake in the middle of the night	40
~~daughter~~	41
relinquish	42
laid out	43

first visitation	46
origin of flight	47
precipice	48
decipher	49
using story to ask for forgiveness	51
underworld **as**	55
three tasks she'll set you complete*	56
early days	57
darkness shapes itself around you	58
terra nova	59
echo chamber	60
no matter how fast	61
still it lurches after you	62
encounter	63
deep time	64
crone **as**	67
preparation for the search	68
she finds you	70
there are places	71
she rarely gets straight to the point	72
mate	73
she lays you down on the forest floor	74
wake in the early hours	75
mother country	76
circumnavigation	77
acknowledgements	79
about the author	80

ex**is**tence

                                                                            th**is** cluster of cells

                    th**is** version of a body

                                      th**is** vantage point

          th**is** sequence of events   *{o agony} {o ecstasy}*

                                th**is** in**s**istence

th**is** circling back

                      th**is** re**sis**tance

        th**is** relinqu**is**hing

                    is

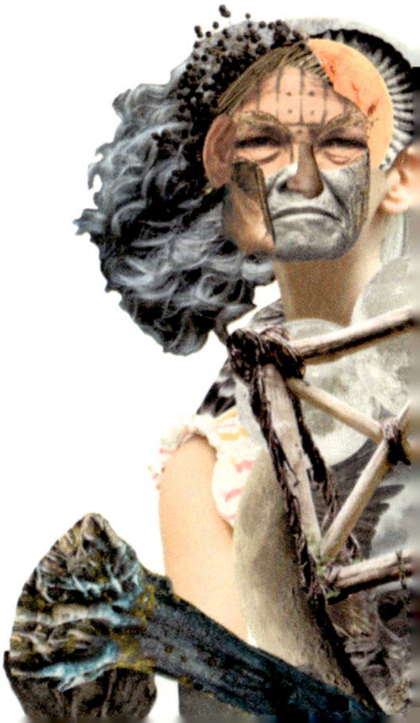

child **as**

> vision **as** origin **as** sapling **as** burden **as** innocence **as** future **as** legacy **as** insatiable **as** singular **as** yearning **as** relentless **as** tender **as** guilt **as** vulnerable **as** parasite **as** anchor **as** sponge **as** instinct **as** boundless **as** pure **as** brazen **as** perfection **as** bruise **as** exhausting **as** exquisite **as** barter **as** link **as** feral **as** mystery **as** measure **as** fragile **as** power **as** punchbag **as** imprint **as** brightness **as** endless **as** accident **as** solace **as** ache

dismantle

    you take them apart

        the female first / remove the clothes / uncover her plastic body

        glassy eyes stare straight ahead / avoiding your gaze

        you start to pull / one leg pops out of the socket / then the other

        arms next / still she won't look at you

        the face / a blank expression / refusing to comply

        the head / takes several yanks / before it yields

        the sexless torso / a final accusation / slips through your hands / falls to the floor

            the male next / the process much the same

            [*though he appears to hold your gaze*]

origin story

      there   (*half of you*) waiting
      three brothers (*half of them*) waiting too
      five others waiting   but you can't see their faces

      you lie in wait   all the unremembered days
      the waiting is warm dark   pulsing infinite worlds

      you're impatient for your father (in a workman's jacket)
      to knock on the door your mother opens

      you're waiting for life to point a finger and decree

          not you
                      not you
you
                                not you
    you
        not you
                             not you
you
        not you... **okay**   you

one of these days

        you'll ask to return

                to liquid darkness
                before the gravitational
                pull of DNA / before the
                victory dance of xx
                over xy

        you'll rest there awhile

    unassigned
        uninterrupted
            suspended in milky silence

n**oti**onal

        bl**oo**d cl**o**ts

              size **of** a fist

                  size **of** a f**o**etus

                      size **of** a fantasy

                          size **of** a l**o**nging

       size **of** a sister

inkling **of** a life (*still*)

            fl**o**ating face d**ow**n in darkness

conjure

one of the five is a girl / your sister / not a real sister / a real sister is complicated / flesh and bone / competition / not a real sister has no need for oxygen / or birth or chronology / she just is / perfectly formed / singular in design and intention / at night in the warm darkness you lie / facing one another / when your eyes close / she is still there / when she closes her eyes / you wait for her return / she comes back doesn't she / if you hold your breath long enough / if you outlast the silence before the fall

a low branch / wide enough for two small bodies / peas in a pod side by side / four legs swinging / light dapples through leaves / dances across two faces

yes it's morning / yes it's always summer

little girl

standing (*still*)

      under the apple tree

                         where you left her

      missing a rib *{sister}*

you stepped   into the world ***[wound]***

                  numb fingers tracing

the jagged *{tender}* line of stitches

when you leave

> she stares at her sandals / to keep her mind from wandering / into danger / white leather t-straps / no scuff marks they come later / her finger traces the line of raised stitches encircling each foot / a consolation / a grounding / small silver buckles gleam / cool to the touch / capable of skin pinching cruelty / if you don't come back / she has the floral motif to explore / one on each sandal / tear shaped petals / existing in negative space

out in the world

always busy aren't you / always something to do / so many people / once or maybe twice / so many faces to scan / the fear it wasn't her / round and round / circling the wound / the fear it was her / once you thought you saw her

meanwhile

    she doesn't grow older   neither
    does she stay the same

    small incremental   shifts
    of perception

    like what she chooses to   focus
    on

    from negative space to   dark
    energy

    gravitational lensing of   galaxy
    clusters

    rotational   speed
    of stars

    that which cannot be   observed
    directly

    only its effect on that   which
    can

    just like me she says aloud to   no
    one

    hoping you   might
    hear

night vision

> you've been here before / not the place / the feeling is what's familiar / this time you are standing in a square / people moving past you / the townhall with its large clock / people moving faster / a wall of water rising up / so high the sky no longer is the sky / that feeling again / wanting to run / wanting to stay / the wall rising higher threatening to engulf / baptise you / an old woman suddenly at your side / taking your hand / mouthing words you strain to hear

my beloved

i have been walking   for days and years

        i have been walking back to you

are you there (still)   is the tree (still) there

don't be scared when you see me

frayed   features blurred   hair the colour of overcast skies

little girl   can i take your soft hand   put it in my side

tell you how sorry i am

        ask to come home

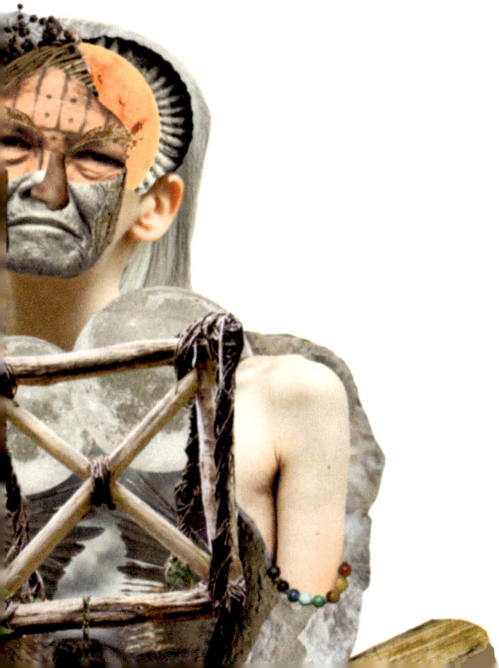

hanging by a thread

>
> what if / in the liquid darkness another had reached the egg / the irresistible pull of that DNA a different song to sway to / xy triumphant / all swan feathers and grace / pirouetting across the dancefloor / xx crestfallen
>
> lays down her dancing shoes / sidesteps into the wings

man **as**

> slain **as** *christ* **as** *judas* **as** son of god **as** risen **as** *herod* **as** sixth hour **as** scourged **as** judgement **as** disciple **as** sleeping **as** thirty gold pieces **as** thief **as** forsaken **as** innocent blood **as** sacrifice **as** king **as** liar **as** *pontius pilate* **as** nail **as** virtuous **as** sword **as** lamb of god **as** vinegar **as** thirst **as** saviour **as** prisoner **as** son of man **as** betrayed **as** centurion **as** calvary **as** sinner **as** high priest **as** pierced side **as** crown of thorns **as** boy child **as** broken body **as** last supper **as** place of the skull

tell me again

        he asks no one in particular

        which part am i meant to be playing now

those boys you used to teach

> how like little gods they were / first year in school / the world had yet to hunt them down / chisel the softness from their cheeks / rip out their open hearts / how when they tired of racing full tilt across the yard / they would seek you out / lean into the comfort / press their cheek against your hand

diviner

> once upon a time the boy with no shadow grew into a man / no imprint on the pillow / no matter how often you laid him down / pressed your ear to his chest / listened to the lament of deep water / starless rivers coursing through darkness

interview

      asked when i knew   the attacks and killings

                                                    had to end

    i told her it was when i held my new born daughter

          cupped her tiny head in my hands

      knew i had to protect her   from everything

   from these fists

              this fucking anger

                                               this shame

prodigal

a decade on / he is sitting at your kitchen table on
the same chair / back from the dead / back from
the edge of endless drought / gone as far north as
a man can go / before ice blooms in his veins

here now / sun through the window on his face
/ the ease of the afternoon / a fatted calf / a feast
in full swing

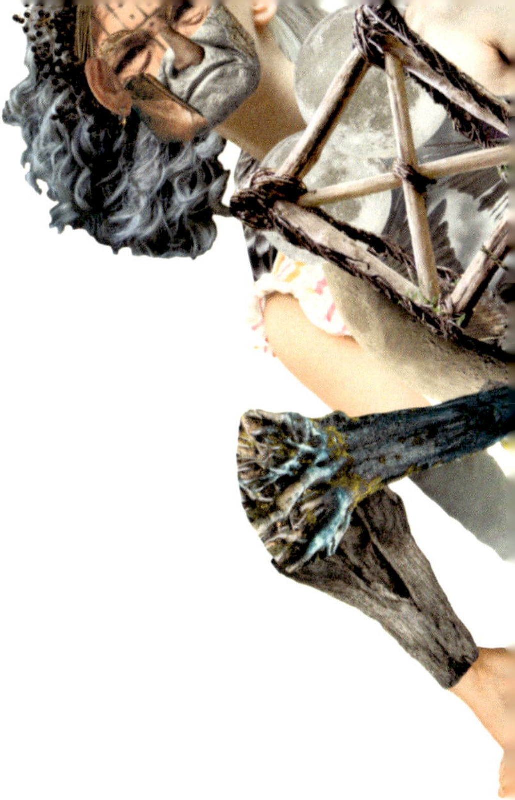

mother **as**

vessel **as** state **as** indentured **as** fulfilment **as** sorrow **as** calling **as** fraught **as** currency **as** *madonna* **as** whole **as** martyr **as** fecund **as** night feed **as** freedom **as** empty nest **as** fertile earth **as** gravitational pull **as** prism as *omphalos* **as** treasure **as** life giver **as** lethal **as** warrior **as** nature **as** terror **as** matriarch **as** breast **as** longing **as** compromise **as** status **as** nurture **as** strength **as** lush **as** vale of tears **as** birthplace **as** battlefield

wake in the middle of the night

clutching your throat

    you've swallowed a key or a ring

its solid mass stuck in your gullet

    beyond your fingers reach

                  how stupid of you to lose it

                this thing (*whatever it is*)

                    that matters so much

you stricken

    you condemned

cast out of the kingdom forever

        this house / this man / these sleeping children

            oblivious to your absence

~~daughter~~

> once upon a time / your
> (*still*) mother / her body
> (*still*) warm to the touch
>
> once upon a time / your
> (*still*) father / his body
> (*still*) warm to the touch
>
>
> static gathering speed / orphaned
> particles hurtling through space

relinquish

> you've seen it done / witnessed how easy it can be / to lay a life down / step back / halt the treatment / turn your face to the wall / close your eyes / beckon death to seep into bones / loosen binds / welcome the oncoming silence / the blurring borders dissolving / rele

laid out

🌑

who do you want to be

                careful how you answer

your mother knew about the illusion of choice / knew no matter what promise the moon made peering out from behind the trees at the bottom of the long garden / in the morning she still woke in the same tired body / throat closed shut / blood seeping through the towel between her legs onto the sheet / the weight of an unspoken life hidden by her careful movements / getting out of bed / making breakfast / dropping the youngest off at school

                    you remember the shadow cast by that weight
                            it carried its own familiar scent
                sometimes you go back to that place / search it out
                      spray it on the tender flesh of your wrist
                            hold it to your nose / drink in
                                    its heavy promise

🌑

who did she want you to be

        careful with the words you place in her mouth

your mother *was* proud of you

        you know that   a matter of fact

                      but there was envy too

she gifted you a spoken life and you reached out and took it from her / then came the distance between the unspoken and the spoken / each syllable each cycle of the moon moving you further apart

> does the word *betray* apply here

> if you placed that word in her mouth
> would it belong there
> would she choose to utter it

she's sitting in the chair to the left of the fireplace / the weight is settled in her lap / its scent seeking you out / you take a step back / then another

> do you feel torn

> in that moment you are neither
> spoken nor unspoken / you belong nowhere

☾

who do you think they want you to be

> careful   they may not like the answer

there are four children's voices speaking over each other

the featherweight of a fifth / a blurred memory of a toilet cubicle / the nurse taking the towel which had been pressed between your legs / her voice echoing off the enamel surfaces / registering what your body had expelled three moon cycles in

> *the fifth voice unspoken once was briefly*
> *a purity to the silence between you*
> *it asks nothing of you   wants nothing from you now*
> *it has no scent*
> *you attach no word to your side of the silence*

the other four

yes / you are their mother / you give them use of that word / allow them to speak it freely / it belongs / doesn't belong to you

        the moon you've left peering through the trees
          at the end of the long back garden

your body   full throated now

    released from all questions

        lays
           itself
              down

first visitation

> there you are / a year on from her death / a year when blurred days and weeks were swallowed whole / there you are numb and raw / but grateful for the time you had with her / and the manner of her passing / now your hand on the threshold door unwilling to push it open / half turned to walk away / when the play of light through leaves / on the tree outside the house begins to speak in patterned tongues

origin of flight

                                        into the still centre of an afternoon / no warning except darkening skies / through the aperture of a dilated pupil / an infinity of birds comes rushing towards you / commanding courtship-kinship-worship of flight muscle / fused clavicle / keeled sternum

                                        all the birds that ever flew across red skies / plummeting towards your world's end

precipice

magpies discover the wood pigeon nest in the tree outside the house / by the time you get there the chicks are lying on the footpath / snow angels / bloodied wings fanning the concrete / heads caved in / a shimmering aura about their broken bodies / soft and yielding when you scoop them up / one first then the other / placing them out of harm's way / reminded of the afternoon when a young magpie flew down the chimney / its panicked attempts at flight / your hands firm around its body / heart beating wildly against the knife's edge

decipher

you kept dreaming of houses

        shapeshifting mansions with warrens of unused rooms
someone left to you years ago but you never claim them
(why won't you claim them)

      or the two places you lived as a child
the flat above the chemist on the main road
    the terraced house where your eldest brother lives still

  sometimes you dream of this house
    a blurred version you can't fit inside

  other nights it's a different house
    crawling through attic space
      convincing yourself this one is bigger
        has more to offer
(your breathing says otherwise)

//

    recently your dreams deposit you onto roads
  like the little swaying man in google maps

always you're in a rush to be elsewhere
  always on the back foot
    (why didn't you prepare)

  now it's the road between your childhood homes
    their location a footnote in the back of your mind

      (you know you didn't leave from here
        & it's not where you're going)

      or it's a dual carriageway
         you're dodging traffic
            or in a car often about to crash

///

you don't know where you're going
   but when you get there
on the rare occasion *there* is reached

  you feel no relief on arrival

     though once you ended up in a room with a baby in a basket
on the floor and knew it was significant

but couldn't fathom why

using story to ask for forgiveness

                in this version you are the woodcutter

you are the woodcutter's wife

you are the dead mother

                      you may also be the witch

    sometimes she is *hansel*

        sometimes she is *gretel*

    sometimes she is their whispers
        in the dark of the hungry night

            for brevity's sake we'll dispense
                with the pebbles and breadcrumbs and crying

always it is six days before her ninth birthday

    always she is thirsty and you don't take heed

always her body's cellular mutiny
    the sickly fruitiness of her breath

        like most stories it goes back to an absent mother

            a fearful father

        a blindsided moon

in one version a parched forest
        crawling on its knees begging for water

    a gingerbread house eating itself from the inside out

        and dry eyed death salivating
rattling her cage

                        trying to sweeten her up

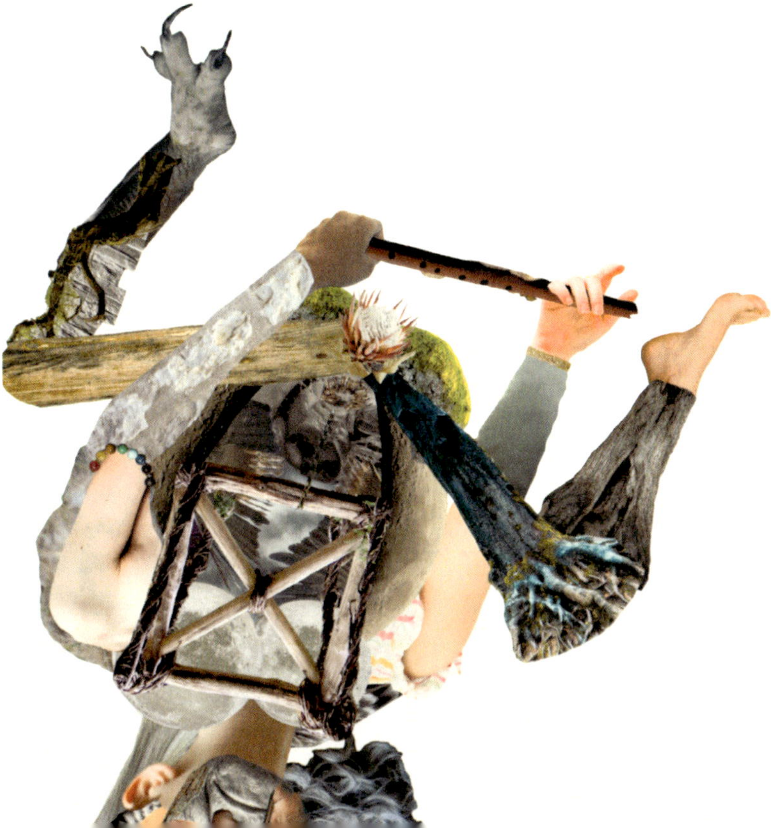

underworld **as**

> entrance **as** descent **as** shelter **as** initiation **as** ritual **as** encounter **as** resting place **as** secret **as** shame **as** fear **as** dormant **as** deposit **as** treasure **as** toxic **as** base **as** hiding place **as** depository **as** narrowing **as** suffocation **as** void **as** seam **as** pressure **as** *dis* **as** mantle **as** core **as** guardian **as** hades **as** solitude **as** oblivion **as** eternity **as** mine **as** tomb **as** vault **as** crypt **as** cave **as** city **as** catacomb **as** labyrinth **as** minotaur **as** nightmare **as** pitch black **as** dead end **as** impenetrable **as** sunless **as** mirror **as** other **as** surrender

three tasks she'll set you to complete*

you must:

        abandon   your life

        travel to » » »   » » » » » »   *you know not where*

you know not what   < < << < <   << << < <   *bring back*

* or she'll roast you whole / suck the marrow from your bones / place burning coals in the sockets of your eyes

early days

                        down here she calls you *persephone* so you might feel at home / she places gifts in your backpack / tubular eyes of an owl / velvet fur of a mole / kinship with the dark

// still fear rises //

                        she calls up *eurydice* / a distant memory of life hovering on the periphery / her soft unhurried movements / human form loosened like rain / quickening pooling into the cupped hands of the darkening earth

// still fear rises //

                        she brings you to the place where all the dead abide / look there / your mother / her mother / her mother / on and on / ancestral seam unravelling back / to the first mother / root and stock / eyes long accustomed to the dark

//   //

darkness shapes itself around you

burrowing inside your brain
probing soft tissue

an underworld unfolds

↓

now an alley / hidden doorways / stench of piss

↓

now a concrete maze / jagged glass embedded in walls / closing in

↓

now a familiar road / crouching shadows / sudden movement

↓

frenzied laughter / hand on a screwdriver / searching for prey

↓

scrape of metal against bone / chasm opening / plunging headlong terra nova

down here

            you hardly recognise yourself

you become skin

            a demarcation

    you become bone

               a grey citadel

       you become blood

                  a subterranean river

down here in the warm dark

                you slip through cracks

   seep through stone

echo chamber

        down here you learn to unspeak / to stifle words that could be used as spells / or easy explanations

        a burial shroud wrapped tightly around your throat and mouth / you venture further in / each turn a keening wraith crouching in the shadows

        cold seeps into your bones / igniting visions of the dead and undead / locked in a terrible embrace / a pulsing half life fumbling its way towards you

do you run

        do you stay

no matter how fast

                                        you run _

      and run _   and run_

and run _   and run _

                    and run_   and run_   and run_

and run_   and run_   *oh god_*

        and run_   and run_   and run_

and run_   and run_

still it lurches after you

                          dragging   its limbs

                                              calling out   your name

encounter

        turn at last to face it / take in the terror in its eyes /
        the unwashed body covered in open sores

{the pity of it} {the suffering of it} {the loneliness of it}

        your arms reaching out to hold / cradle / your tears
        flowing / its tears flowing / together laying down
        in the darkness / sleep for a thousand years / dream
        of shallow graves / wake / weep / comfort / sleep
        for a thousand years / dream of morning / wake as
        one / clear skinned / clear eyed / hungry for home

deep time

                                        when asked how long you stayed below

you tell them

        long enough

                    to find a way back

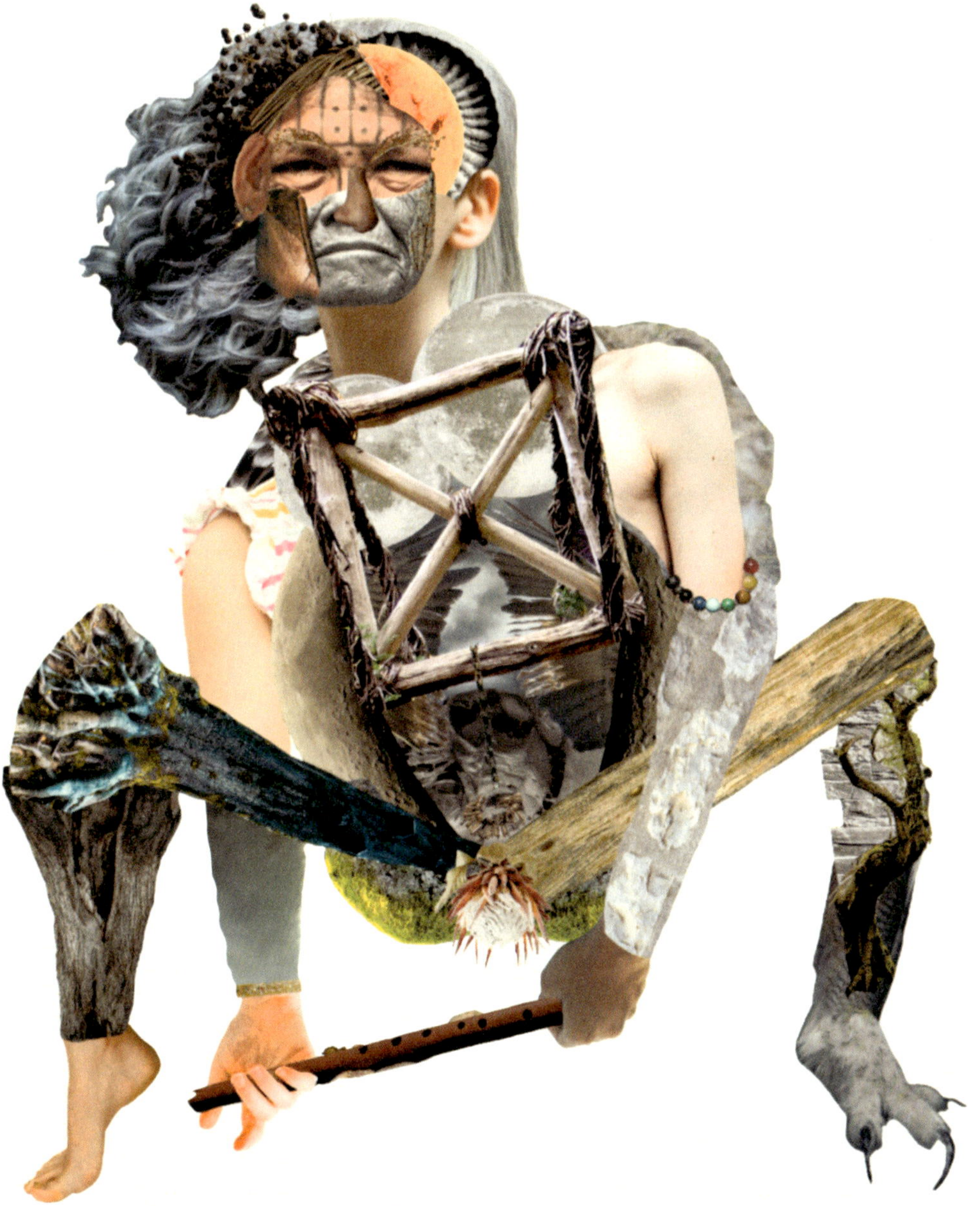

crone **as**

> thin place **as** wolf **as** reckoning **as** silence **as** scar **as** remedy **as** forest **as** ample **as** hollow **as** weathered **as** wintering **as** question **as** portent **as** midwife **as** deathbed **as** dusk **as** scar **as** shadow **as** shapeshifter **as** *criatura* **as** umbilicus **as** feral **as** resistance **as** field **as** liminal **as** circle of chalk **as** ear to the ground **as** gap in the hedge **as** fossil **as** veil **as** stubborn **as** undergrowth **as** dried blood **as** fuel **as** hunger **as** worn track **as** pilgrim **as** red sky

preparation for the search

take a length of string
two plastic cups
something sharp
to make a hole in the bottom of each

when you've made the holes
(careful not to pierce skin)
feed the length of string through each cup
knotting each end

place one cup to your ear
keeping the string taut

tell me   what do you hear
the sea the wind
her voice rushing towards you

//

feast on silence for forty days and forty nights
until their name calling no longer touches you

obedient child

                      dutiful mother

                                          little woman

//

smear your face with soot

//

a hand drawn map of places
you're likely to find her

                                                             down the end of the garden
                                                                    grubbing for worms

the morning after
laying out the body

                                        in the old country
                                   at the bottom of a lake

                                                             play wrestling wolf pups
                                                             at the entrance to the cave

hunkered down
waiting for the head to crown

                                       //

dress for snowstorms   scorched earth   swollen rivers

dress like you're never coming back

                                       //

when you find her call out

   crone   *cailleach*   *baba yaga*   *loba*

       wild woman   *old mother death*

but she'll only answer to your name

                                         //

take me with you

she finds you

        weeping in a corner / squats down / takes your hand / she's got all day / all night if that's what it takes / for an opening

    how to bear it when it's always been so

        kin   killing   kin

    a machete   a gas oven   a mushroom cloud

        hunger stones   grass stained mouths   silent villages

a face punched   a throat bruised   a voiceless woman

    a noose   a burning cross   a cheering crowd

a hardening   a shutting down   a turning away

        your hand in her calloused hand / dawn seeping into a blood red sky / clouds gathering / a turning towards there are places

                    she will not take you / not yet / only she can travel to where kin fell / in filthy rags / wasted bodies so light the earth received them like rain / absolved them of their terrible hunger

forty days and forty nights

                    she crouches amongst stones and furrows / matted hair sunken eyes / loosened skin / shivering / muttering each family name in the old tongue / keening / calling forth / fusing rounded flesh to bone

to atone

                    she kneels before the hazel grove / the sacred hawthorn / stands in the place where the sessile oak grows within ruined walls of the cottage / bows to the empty *cailleach* / lays herself down in the hearth / smears her face with soot / begs for forgiveness she rarely gets straight to the point

       patience she reminds you
          her hair a tangled nest of twigs and leaves
       all the good stuff takes time

                        the earth's crust hardening / slow shifting continents / the time it rained for two million years / the heavens opening / the earth's upturned face / throat a river mouth of quenched desire

mate

                she's wild about him / her hairy man / *iron john* / shapeshifter / on top of her / sky father / beneath her / earth father / bedded down in the nourishing dark / licking / nipping / wolf fangs grinning she lays you down on the forest floor

        you / foster child / raised by a city thriving on neglect / smell of hops / belch of car fumes / a dirty river / a cluster of houses / a curved road cracked grey concrete / rusted railings / sunlight glinting off rain streaked windows

        you / transported / eyes shut / back pressed against the mulch of leaves / fallen branches / crumbling bark / arms outstretched across bracken / spongy moss / fingertips tracing lichen whorls

        you / refusing to open your eyes / turn your head / for fear of capsizing / afraid to succumb to wood sorrel / wild garlic / yellow pimpernel / drown in the violet of bluebells / sink deeper / never go back

wake in the early hours

to a sound coming from the long back garden

leave the warmth of **your** bed   head out into the cold night air

find **her** crouched under a full moon   digging a hole

kneel beside **her**

feel a sharp lump in **your** throat   retch into **her** cupped hands

a key   a ring   wet and glistening

she places them in the hole   pressing them into soft earth

for safekeeping **she** says

you stand up   wait for the moon to give the nod

then off with the **pair of you**

into the wide world

mother country

she asks if you ever miss it

surfacing a memory / an afternoon in spring / the four of them running ahead to the playground / the sky darkening / a sudden storm / hailstones bouncing off the path / the grass / their exposed skin / the forever it took to get back home / your body a shield too small to stop their cries / fumbling to open the front door / the calm of the house / racing up the stairs / wet clothes discarded / five snug bodies in the bed / pink and drowsy / the afternoon a lost adventure / a once upon a time

circumnavigation

right so she says and off you traipse

down the narrow road that leads to the field where the chestnut horse is grazing / the curve of the bay to the left / straight ahead the swell of the mountain / above you the late morning sun / in the fields about / tall feathered grasses / clustered buttercups / hedges of dog roses / into the silence drops the drone of a bee / the sound of a car in the distance

who knew the world could be this big she says before you head off / across the headland / taking the long way round

Acknowledgements

Thanks to the editors of the following publications, programmes or websites in which some of the poems, or versions of the poems, first appeared:
Banshee Lit, HOWL New Irish Writing, Eat the Storms Poetry Podcast, Cultivating Voices and *New Normal Culture: Keywords*.

Thank you:

To The Arts Council of Ireland for their generous bursary award (2022), which gave me the time and space to complete the first draft of this collection. To Poetry Ireland, DCU and the Adrian Brinkerhoff Poetry Foundation, who, through their Poet-in-Residence Award, gifted me time to edit and complete the final manuscript. To Dublin City Council for their literature bursary award (2023).

To Jessie Lendennie and Siobhán Hutson Jeanotte at Salmon Poetry for their love and commitment to poetry. To Darragh Murphy (aj_axis) for his cover artwork. To my Friday Poetry group: Fióna Bolger, Alvy Carragher, Srilata K and Özgecan Kesici-Ayoubi, for their love and feedback. To Jess Traynor for her mentoring support and kind words about the collection, and to Luke Morgan, Alice Kinsella and Tapasya Narang for their generous words. To Claire Murphy, Frank Jordan, Jenn Little, Fióna Bolger and Eithne Lannon for their feedback on earlier drafts of the collection. To Alvy Carragher for her tireless editorial support throughout and to Stephen Murphy for his eagle eyes. To Gina Whelan and Shay Maguire for gifting me a week's writing at their house in Louisburgh, where I wrote some of the poems. And finally, to my family, past, present and future. Everything comes back to you.

ANNE TANNAM has published three poetry collections, *Take This Life* (Wordonthestreet Publishers 2011), *Tides Shifting Across My Sitting Room Floor* (Salmon Poetry 2017) and *Twenty-six Letters of a New Alphabet*, (Salmon 2021). She is the current Poet in Residence with Poetry Ireland (2023-2025). She was awarded a Literature Bursary from the Arts Council of Ireland in 2022 and from Dublin City Council in 2023. For more on her poetry, visit www.annetannampoetry.ie. Anne is also a Professional Certified Coach who helps writers design and sustain flourishing writing practices. For the past 35 years she's mentored and facilitated and regularly runs workshops and clinics nationwide and internationally. For more on Anne's coaching, visit www.creativecoaching.ie

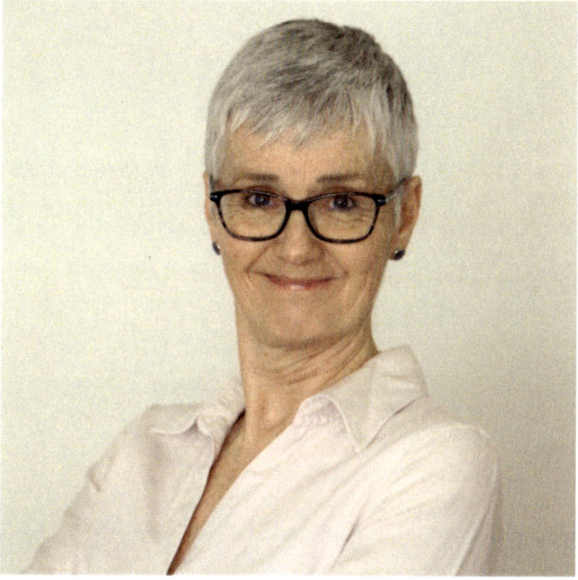

salmonpoetry

Cliffs of Moher, County Clare, Ireland

"Publishing the finest Irish and international literature."
Michael D. Higgins, President of Ireland